Photography copyright © 1989 by Katsuhiko Tokunaga.

English language edition published in the United States
by Howell Press, Inc., 700 Harris Street, Charlottesville,
Virginia 22901. Telephone (804) 977-4006.
All rights reserved.

Printed in Italy

Library of Congress Catalog Card Number 88-62457

ISBN 0-943231-16-7

HOWELL PRESS

preface by
gianfranco da forno

TOP
TEAMS

photography by
katsuhiko tokunaga

*T*hose magnificent men in their flying machines...

During the barnstorming days of early aviation, pilots thrilled audiences with their death-defying, daredevil performances. A kick to the wheels, a jump into the cockpit, a signal to the mechanic to turn the propeller, an unstable taxi down the grass, and a leap into the freedom of the sky to perform risky maneuvers gave pilots personal satisfaction. Conquering the skies was an experience that few aviators ever tired of and one that was always new and challenging.

Today, the romance of aviation's early days has given way to new technology, a new breed of daring pilots. Aircraft can now travel twice the speed of sound, take off and land from platforms in the middle of the ocean, and carry payloads as heavy as the airplane itself. In fact, flight techniques and equipment have changed so much over the years that flying has become an expensive game. Training jet pilots costs governments and private institutions a fortune. Money is also needed to study more responsive G-suits, which keep pilots from losing consciousness; light helmets are mandatory on half-hour jet flights, which are as physically demanding and stressful as nine hours of manual labor or 10 hours of office work. In the past skilled pilots outperformed their airplanes; now, many airplanes can outperform the best trained aviators.

Today's barnstormer is the pilot who performs dangerous aerobatic maneuvers in jet formations high above the earth. Such synchronized flying requires that each pilot follow an intricate path, involving split-second timing. Pilots must memorize subtle variations in flight parameters during a formation's loops and rolls, join-ups and separations. Weather conditions, local topography, obstructions unique to each airshow site, varying lengths and widths of runways, local and international flight regulations, and necessary safety precautions further complicate the aerobatic pilot's job. Discipline, practice, experience, and pilot aptitude are all key ingredients for aerobatic teams to achieve extraordinary performances.

The Top Teams featured here are the seven premiere aerobatic teams in the world. Each one is the «flying ambassador» of its country, demonstrating abroad the national spirit and tradition of its homeland. Great rapport between nations has been established by these unofficial diplomats, who demonstrate that their countries have the ability to train and develop superb air forces. Their esprit de corps and the perfection, beauty, and harmony of their work reflect well upon their homelands.

Goodwill, affection, and understanding between people of different nations are the legacy of the barnstorming tradition, perpetuated today by «these magnificent men in their flying machines».

Gianfranco Da Forno

As the result of my activities as an aviation photographer over the past year, I have taken 37 flights on military high-performance jets - a total of 51 hours.

In some months I made no flights, while in other months I flew three flights a day. This averages out to about one flight every 10 days, which is small when compared to the flight time of professional pilots, but significant for a civilian photographer. It took me almost 10 times longer to obtain permission to fly with the various military organizations than I actually spent in the air. Considering the time I spent securing permission, I suppose the number of times I was able to fly was a high for a freelance photographer.

It is important to work not only as an artistic photographer, who strives to take one perfect shot, but as a photojournalist, who thoroughly covers the subject by taking pictures on the ground or by interviewing pilots with a tape-recorder in hand. I am interested in photojournalism and will take shots on the ground, but since high-performance jets fly in three-dimensional space, it goes without saying that taking air-to-air shots is the best way to capture the essence of jet aviation. In a sense, shooting in the air is indispensable to good aviation photography.

For example, if you think of an airliner flying between two points, you wouldn't deny that the climax of its flight would be its taking off and landing. On the other hand, if you think of a military high-performance jet, you see its takeoffs and landings as mere prologues and epilogues to its actual flight. Military high-performance jets must endure heavy G-forces in air-combat maneuvers. Sometimes they fly low across the terrain and encounter turbulence. These types of dynamic conditions cannot be shot from the ground. That is why taking air-to-air photographs is the only way in which a photographer can capture the essence of military jet flight.

Taking shots only from the ground means that you take shots as a stranger. Air-to-air shots make you intimate with the jet's operation. The pilot and photographer must work closely together. Some aviation photographers, who usually rely on the help of assistants, find air-to-air shooting troublesome, because there is no space for an assistant in the cockpit. They must do all the work themselves. I find the process very exciting – doing briefings, making plans for taking specific shots, photographing jets while experiencing Gs, and completing the shooting. The pilot and photographer do all they can in order to «take good shots». If they succeed, they enjoy sharing their success.

Unfortunately, when you are shooting military aircraft, there are limits to what you can do in the air. This is understandable. It is difficult for any nation's air force to permit a foreign journalist on their latest, most powerful military jets. Many such jets are equipped with advanced technologies that the military does not want revealed. Even on jets that contain few military secrets, it is not unusual to be given less than 10 minutes to take pictures. That is usually the amount of spare time available between training sorties. The worst thing that can happen is when you find out that your jet has used up most of its fuel in training and only has enough to get back to base. In those cases you never get the chance to take interesting pictures, and it is hard to keep from feeling frustrated. Many opportunities to shoot air-to-air occur only once, so even with an air force's permission, it is uncertain whether or not you'll be able to accomplish anything.

The aerobatic teams featured here are magnificent subjects that enabled me to fulfill my ideals of air-to-air photography. These colorful jets are photogenic. They are exceptional examples of military aircraft designed for «show». In a big formation, they perform loops and rolls which only high-performance military jets can do. They are the ultimate subjects for me as an aviation photographer. No other aircraft give you more climactic moments than high-performance jets when you are taking air-to-air shots. Watching aerobatic teams, even from the ground, is exciting. When you shoot their performance from the air, you pulls Gs continuously, which is rather hard on your body. But after taking shots of an aerobatic show in full sequence, you also feel exhilarated, because you understand that you have completed a great photographic assignment.

I have been flying and taking pictures with 10 aerobatic teams from nine countries for the past eight years. In this book, you will find the seven main aerobatic teams. Usually, when I make a book like this, I choose the photographs by myself. This time, I requested the assistance of Lt. Col. Gianfranco Da Forno of Frecce Tricolori, the aerobatic team of the Italian Air Force. People who are familiar with my work may find these images a little different from the ones I've shot in the past. But I am satisfied with them because Gianfranco, an individual who is part of a prominent aerobatic team, kindly helped me choose the photographs he felt were the best representations of aerobatic flight. I hope you enjoy *Top Teams* and feel the attraction these aerobatic teams possess.

My friend Gianfranco has not only been in charge of the public affairs office of Frecce Tricolori for eight years, but he is also well known as a historian of the aerobatic teams of the world. He understands my photographs, and his family and mine are good friends. I am proud to be able to create this book with a professional like him. I am glad that a friendship between an Italian and a Japanese helped produce *Top Teams*. I would also like to express my deep gratitude to Mr. René Leonarduzzi of Magnus Edizioni, who worked both as producer and director for this book.

Katsuhiko Tokunaga

AERONAUTICA MILITARE ITALIANA

FRECCE TRICOLORI

Aerobatic flying has played an important role in the Italian Air Force pilot training program. By learning to fly in aerobatic formations, pilots developed confidence in themselves and learned the capabilities of their aircraft.

A military pilot must be an athlete first if he wishes to man his aircraft in combat situations with maximum efficiency and full control. Consequently, aerobatic flying is the offshoot of strict and constant daily training in air combat maneuvers and interceptions.

In 1930 Colonel Rino Corso Fougier, Commander of the 1st Wing of the Italian Air Force in Udine, Italy, began training pilots to fly aerobatically in formations of five. Other fighter wings adopted similar programs, but World War II ended such training, as pilots were called into battle. When the war ended, formation flying began again, this time with jet aircraft. The 2nd, 4th, 5th, 6th, and 51st Fighter Wings formed a team that represented the Italian Air Force in airshows around Italy and abroad. Teams named Black Lancers, Rampling-Horse, Thunderjets, Red Devils, and White Tigers became legendary.

At the end of 1960, the Air Force decided to form the 313th Aerobatic Training Squadron, dedicated to aerobatic flying, but with the ability to engage in air combat if needed. On July 1, 1961, the squadron was officially inaugurated as the Frecce Tricolori, meaning «three-colored arrows». Since then the team has flown more than 1,500 airshows, visiting all the western European nations, the Middle East, Africa, Canada, and the United States. Everywhere they go, they show the expertise of the men and aircraft of the Italian Air Force.

To be part of the Frecce Tricolori, a pilot must have at least 1,000 flying hours. All personnel are recruited from various units of the Air Force and chosen after undergoing a rigorous screening process, necessary because of the high degree of responsibility and professionalism required of Frecce Tricolori pilots.

To date, 72 pilots, 4 public affairs/commentator officers, and 5 technical officers, plus 150 crewmen, have passed through the gates of Rivolto's «Mario Visintini» Airport.

The team flew the North American F-86E Sabre until 1963, when the first Italian-built aircraft, the Aeritalia-Fiat G-91PAN, joined the team. In 1981 the old «Gina» was replaced by the Aermacchi MB-339A/PAN, a true gem of the Italian aerospace industry. Conceived as a trainer, the aircraft is used at the Air Force flying school. It is reliable, and records show that the squadron has obtained an aircraft availability in excess of 95 percent during the airshow seasons.

The Frecce Tricolori fly a formation of nine aircraft. There is also a solo that does more than fill up the empty spaces left by the formation. A performance by the solo is literally a show within a show, with the soloist doing maneuvers such as the «lomçovák». Czechoslovakian for «drunken man», tail slide and spin, no other jet can do.

The team performs three different programs, depending on the cloud ceiling and visibility. Pilots stay with the team for three to five years.

The Frecce Tricolori formation: Pony 1 - Leader, Pony 2 - First left wingman, Pony 3 - First right wingman, Pony 4 - Second left wingman, Pony 5 - Second right wingman, Pony 6 - First slot, Pony 7 - Third left wingman, Pony 8 - Third right wingman, Pony 9 - Second slot, Pony 10 - Solo. The Commander, Pony 0, is the only replacement available to the team; he replaces the leader if it becomes necessary.

ROYAL AIR FORCE

RED ARROWS

The jewel of the Royal Air Force (RAF) and the pride of the British people, the Red Arrows are descendants of the many teams that have flown the English skies since the 1920s.

Following on the heels of the Yellowjacks, a 1964 team from Flight Training School Number 4, the Red Arrows were established on March 1965 in Fairford, England, as a detachment of the Central Flying School. Their first Commander-Leader was Lieutenant Lee Jones, former leader of the Yellowjacks and pilot of the Black Arrows. They flew seven Gnats their first year, expanded to nine aircraft in 1966, dropped to seven again after moving to Kembie in 1967, and returned to nine aircraft in 1968. An unfortunate loss of pilots and aircraft in 1971 left their formation with seven Gnats once again, but in 1972 two more planes were added.

The team switched from the Gnat, which had flown in a total of 1,070 shows, to the Hawk in 1980. Since the Red Arrows were founded, 30 Gnats had been flown. This high number was due to the replacement of older planes and the loss of planes in accidents. This same year, the Red Arrows moved from Kemble to Scampton.

The Red Arrows' program consists of nine aircraft flying with continuous changes in formation shape. In flight the Synchro Pair (Numbers 6 and 7 in the formation) leave the group and perform their own program, while the remainder of the formation flies split maneuvers.

With beautiful executions, the Red Arrows make impressive low-altitude passes and perform spectacular solos. The team, a standard RAF squadron, demonstrate that the skills and qualities demanded of all RAF officers and enlisted personnel can be put to use even in peacetime. Like the other major aerobatic teams around the world, the Red Arrows can quickly transform into a combat-operational squadron should it become necessary. All Red Arrow pilots come from fighter units of the RAF and are assigned to the aerobatic team for two or three years. New pilots arrive just before the present year's show season ends and begin practicing formation flying immediately.

As a rule, winter training begins with pilots practicing small formations, as often as four times a day, and gradually building up to formations of nine aircraft. Each practice flight is recorded on video so that it can be carefully studied and analyzed. This helps the team achieve perfection in the shortest possible time. To take advantage of better weather conditions, the team conducts some training flights on Cyprus Island in the eastern Mediterranean. Red Arrows perform at approximately 80 airshows each year.

The Red Arrows formation: Red 1 - Leader/commander, Red 2 - First right wingman, Red 3 - First left wingman, Red 4 - Second right wingman, Red 5 - Second left wingman, Red 6 - Synchro pair leader and first slot, Red 7 - Synchro pair two and second slot, Red 8 - Third right wingman, Red 9 - Third left wingman. There is also a team manager who is in charge of the commentary during airshows.

U.S. NAVY

BLUE ANGELS

The official U.S. Navy Flight Demonstration Team was established in 1946, when the chief of naval operations organized and directed a Flight Exhibition Team within the Naval Air Advanced Training Command in Jacksonville, Florida.

Originally called the Lancers, the team changed its name at the end of 1946 to the Blue Angels, apparently in honor of a bar in New York state that the pilots had patronized after an airshow. Lieutenant Commander Roy M. «Butch» Voris was their first leader.

The Blue Angels flew four Grumman F6F-5 Hellcats and a SNJ AT-6 Texan painted to look like a Japanese Zero fighter. Their program consisted of a dogfight between the formation and the Zero, which was always «shot» down at the end of the performance.

The Zero was equipped with a smoke device that simulated being hit. A dummy Japanese pilot «parachuted» to the ground and was immediately captured by a squad of Marines. The way in which the Blue Angels flew their diamond formation and their «roll in trail» during these shows soon became their signature.

At the end of 1946 another aircraft was assigned to the team – the Grumman F8F-1 C/D Bearcat. This aircraft was superseded by the F9F-2 Panther in 1949 and the F9F-8 Cougar six years later. In 1957 the short-nosed Grumman F11F-1 Tiger joined the team, soon to be replaced by the long-nosed F11A version. It was followed by the McDonnell Douglas F-4J Phantom II in 1969 and the McDonnell Douglas A-4F Skyhawk in 1974. The A-4F was used for 12 years by the Blue Angels because it was so reliable. Sailors nicknamed the airplane Scooter, Tinker Toy, and Midnight Midget.

In 1987 the Blue Angels adopted the latest aerospace masterpiece – the McDonnell Douglas F/A-18A Hornet. This jet is capable of traveling in excess of Mach 2 speeds. The first of the new generation of modern fighters, it features advanced technologies, such as high angle-of-attack maneuvering capabilities, a controlled dynamic stall, and future applications of thrust-vectoring engines. Since they were established, the Blue Angels have flown more than 2,500 airshows all over the world.

Blue Angel tradition states that the Commander/Leader is always nicknamed «Boss», while the other pilots keep their present call names. One unusual aspect of the team is that they have established firm rules for replacing pilots. The Blue Angel formation and rules: 1 - Commander/Leader (a Navy pilot who changes every odd year); 2 - Right wingman (a Marine pilot who changes every even year); 3 - Left wingman (who will fly in the Number 4 slot the second year); 6 - Solo (who will fly at Number 5 lead solo the second year); 7 - Commentator (who will become either Number 3 or Number 6); 8 - Team Coordinator (a naval flight officer who changes every even year). The formation is made up of six aircraft; Number 7, the Commentator, flies outside the formation; 4 - Slot (is flown by the pilot flying as number 3 in the preceeding season); 5 - Lead Solo (is flown by the pilot flying the opposing solo - nr. 6 - the preceeding season. As a matter of fact every year there is an entry relative to either number 1 or 2 and two entries as 3 and 6).

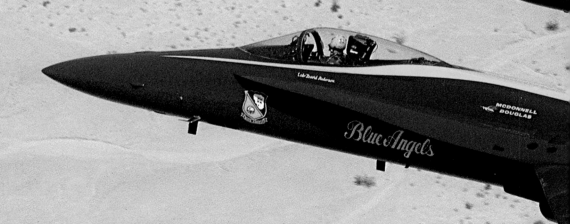

U.S. AIR FORCE

THUNDERBIRDS

On June 1, 1953, the 3600th Air Demonstration Team was officially established. Its home base at the time was Luke Airfield in Arizona.

The team was named «Thunderbirds», a choice influenced by the strong Indian culture of that region. Indian lore told of giant birds that flapped their wings and rapidly blinked their eyes, thereby creating thunder and lightning. Thunderstorms were great battles fought between these thunderbirds and predatory monsters in a fight between good and evil. Thought to resemble gigantic hawks or eagles, thunderbirds were depicted in the art of southwestern American Indians in colors of red, white, and blue. The air demonstration team has used these colors on their aircraft since they were established. The Thunderbirds began flying Republic F-84G Thunderjets, a term which probably also affected the choice of a team name. With their F-84Gs, the team flew a program that lasted 15 minutes and consisted of a series of precision formation aerobatic maneuvers.

By 1955 the team began flying the more modern Republic F-84F Thunderstreak and increased the length of their program to 19 minutes. North American F-100C Supersabres were adopted by the Thunderbirds in May 1956, and the team moved to Nellis, Nevada.

A new aircraft, the very heavy fighter-bomber Republic F-105B-15-RE Thunderchief, was introduced in 1964, but major problems with the aircraft caused the team to go back to the more reliable Supersabre D series. This aircraft was flown by the team for 13 show seasons until November 1968.

Early in 1969 the Thunderbirds completed their conversion to the McDonnell-Douglas F-4E Phantom II. Modifications were made to the Phantoms: dummy Sparrow missiles containing smoke oil were mounted, and the J-79 engines were modified so that pilots could ignite the afterburner section of the engine at a lower power setting.
The Phantoms were flown by the Thunderbirds until November 1973.

In the following year the Thunderbirds switched to the Northrop T-38A Talon. Since it could not be refueled in flight, the Talon prevented the team from traveling beyond the United States and Canada. Nevertheless, the jet stayed with the team until 1982, when a tragic accident killed every Thunderbird pilot except the man flying solo. In October 1982 new pilots and a new airplane, the General Dynamics F-16A Fighting Falcon, put the team back in action. With these F-16As, also called «electric jets», the Thunderbirds could go on the road again, since the jets were capable of in-flight refueling and therefore able to cross oceans. In 1984 the Thunderbirds toured Europe, in 1987 the Far East.

The Thunderbirds are composed of 15 officers and 115 enlisted personnel. Applications for positions on the team are carefully examined. Only the most outstanding individuals are accepted. Pilots stay with the team for three years. If it became necessary, the Thunderbirds, part of a standard U.S. Air Force squadron, would be assigned to first-line combat units. Within 72 hours, their F-16s can be repainted and reconfigured as lethal, combat-ready jets.

The Thunderbirds formation: 1 - Leader/Commander, 2 - Left Wing, 3 - Right Wing, 4 - Slot, 5 - Lead Solo, 6 - Opposing Solo.

ARMÉE DE L'AIR

PATROUILLE DE FRANCE

Flying aerobatic formations has been a tradition in France since 1931, when the first Patrouille d'Étampes was formed with three Morane 230s led by Captain Edouard Amouroux. The Patrouille Weisser, flying the Morane 325 and the Spad 510, soon followed. This impressive aerobatic heritage also included French pioneer aviator Adolphe Pégoud, who was the first pilot to loop-the-loop in a public demonstration in 1913.

After World War II aerobatic flying recommenced. The 2nd, 3rd, and 4th Wings of the French Air Force, the Armée de l'Air, formed teams and flew the DeHavilland DH-100 Vampire and the Republic F-84G Thunderjet. Located in Paris, the 3rd Wing became the official Patrouille de France in 1953. The following year the name was transferred to the 2nd Wing, based in Dijon, which operated French-built Ouragans. From 1955 until 1963, the Patrouille de France name was shared between several aerobatic teams: the Cambrai-based 12th Wing, flying Ouragans and Mystère IVs; the Bremgarten-based 4th Wing, flying Ouragans; the Dijon-based 2nd Wing, now flying Mystère IVs in formations of 5, 7, and 12; and the Nancy-based 7th Wing, flying seven Mystère IVs.

On February 10, 1964, the French Minister of Defense pronounced the Salon-de-Provence flying school heir to all teams formerly known as the Patrouille de France. Since then, the school has been the aerobatic team's home. Fouga Magister CM-170s in formations of six, nine, and 11 were flown until 1980. This pattern was unusual, since nine aircraft, or seven plus two solo aircraft, was the standard formation grouping at the time. Flying Fougas, the Patrouille de France performed at 810 air shows, before switching to seven Alpha jets in 1981 and eight Alphas in 1982. Today's standard formation is six, plus two solos.

Pilots and specialists with the Patrouille de France come from various fighter wings of the French Air Force and remain with the team for three years. They average 35 to 45 shows each year.

The Patrouille de France formation: Athos 1 - Leader/Commander, Athos 2 - Équipier intérieur droit (right internal wingman), Athos 3 - Équipier intérieur gauche (left internal wingman), Athos 4 - Premier charognard (first slot), Athos 5 - Équipier extérieur gauche (left outer wingman), Athos 6 - Équipier extérieur droit (right outer wingman), Athos 7 - Deuxieme charognard (second slot), Athos 8 - Équipier arrière droit et solo (back right wingman and solo), and Athos 9 - Équipier arrière gauche et solo (back left wingman and solo).

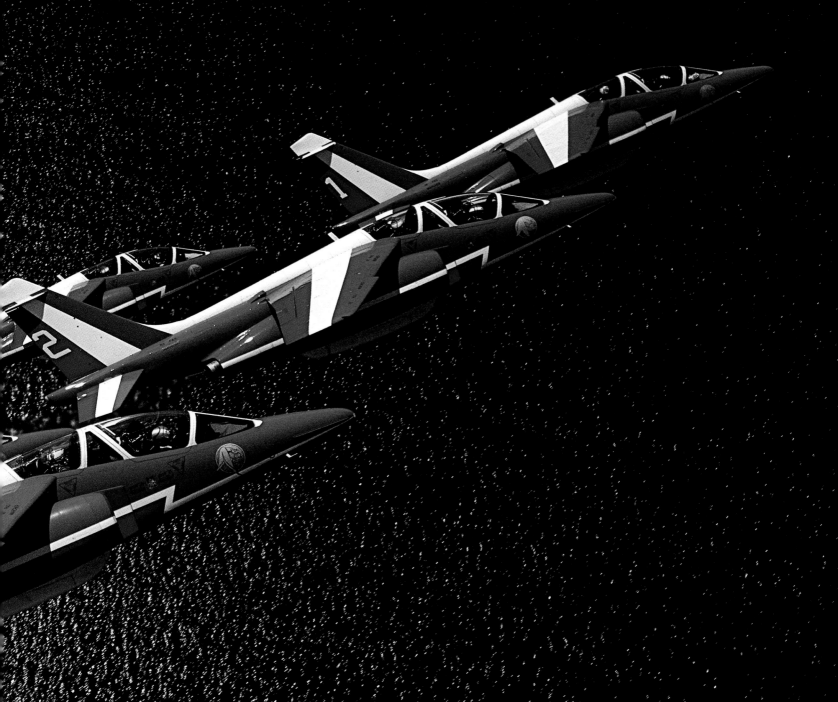

JAPAN AIR
SELF DEFENCE FORCE

BLUE IMPULSE

In 1958 in Hamamatsu, the home of the 1st Wing of the Japan Air Self-Defense Force (JASDF), two flight instructors – Majors Ken Nagasawa and Atstumi Jnada – began flying aerobatic formations at high altitude. Nagasawa had been to Nellis Air Force Base, Nevada, where he had been impressed by the Thunderbirds, the U.S. Air Force aerobatic team stationed there.

All JASDF wings were commissioned after World War II. The 1st Wing was going to be activated on October 19, 1958, and the wing commander decided that the two majors would fly an aerobatic program during the inaugural ceremony. Just before their first public appearance, another pilot, Captain Norio Matsuo, was added. Their call sign was «Checker Blue», after the checkered tops on the tails of their North American F-86F Sabre jets. While the three aviators were a success, the team was disbanded.

In 1959 the 1st Wing was reactivated. The team added Captain Hikaru Nishi as their fourth pilot, flew in two airshows, and then disbanded a second time. December of that year proved to be a significant month for the inactive aerobatic team, because the Thunderbirds visited Japan for the first time. The JASDF staff was so impressed with the American team and their North American F-100Ds that they decided to sanction an official Japanese aerobatic team under the name Airborne Tactics Evaluation Team. Their call sign was changed to «Tenryu», the name of a river near the Hamamatsu airfield. Technical personnel at the base designed a smoke plan for the F-86Fs and repainted them.

Now flying with five pilots, the aerobatic team performed at 13 shows in 1960. Their jets used white smoke and the team adopted the name Impulse Blue. From 1961 to 1965 they flew in an average of 19 shows a year. In 1965 the official name was changed by the JASDF to Tactics Evaluation Team.

After being flown in 545 airshows, the F-86F performed for its last audience on February 8, 1981, at the Iruma Air Base in Tokyo. It was replaced by the Japanese-built Mitsubishi T-2 trainer, and the team relocated to Matsushima air base. An accident in 1982 grounded the team until July 27, 1984, when it once again flew in a national airshow.

Instructor pilots make up the team, which flies between 20 and 30 shows per season, beginning each September. There are six aircraft – four in formation and two solos. While Blue Impulse has never flown outside Japan, their flying style is similar to that of the North American teams.

The Blue Impulse formation: 1 - Leader/Commander, 2 - Left Wing, 3 - Right Wing, 4 - Slot, 5 - Lead Solo, 6 - Opposing Solo.

CANADIAN ARMED
FORCES

SNOWBIRDS

The Snowbirds were conceived in 1971 at Moose Jaw, Saskatchewan, but for seven years the team faced budget constraints, and their survival was uncertain. Finally, in 1978, the Canadian Air Command recognized that a national aerobatic team would have strong promotional value, encouraging communication between Canada and other countries. Their fate was secure.

With the determination and supervision of Colonel Obie Philp, former commander of the Golden Centennaires, the first team was formed in 1971 using pilot-instructors from the Canadian Air Force flying school. The team, comprising seven Canadair CT-114 Tutors in formation, plus one solo, flew in 27 shows that year and in 25 shows the year following. By then another solo aircraft had been added to the team, for a total of nine planes. A contest was held to give the team a name. The winning entry, «Snowbirds», played off the name of Canada's beautiful white buntings.

The year 1974 was a big one for the Snowbirds. Changes were made in the team's formation pattern. The aircraft were painted red, white, and blue, colors still in use today. The team performed in 80 shows, and the Snowbirds broke a record by flying north of the Arctic Circle to Inuvik, a remote outpost in the Canadian Northwest Territories. A year later the Snowbirds flew back to Inuvik, only this time, they flew at midnight.

In September 1977 the Snowbirds were officially named the Canadian Forces Air Demonstration Team. Seven months later, they became the 431st Air Demonstration Squadron. The original 431st had been a bombing squadron during World War II. Nicknamed Hatiten Ronterios, meaning «Sky Warriors», the first 431st Iroquois squadron had been disbanded in 1946.

The Snowbirds fly an average of 70 shows per year, traveling with no support aircraft. Each CT-114 Tutor aircraft carries a pilot, a specialist, and support and publicity material packed in various pockets of the airframe.

Pilots rotate into the team every two years. Ever since the Frecce Tricolori of Italy made their historic appearance in Canadian skies in 1986, the Snowbirds have used colored smoke in their flying programs.

The Snowbird formation: Snowbirds 1 - Commanding Officer/Team Lead (Commandant/Chef d'Équipe), Snowbirds 2 - Inner right wing (Ailier droit intérieur), Snowbirds 3 - Inner left wing (Ailier gauche intérieur), Snowbirds 4 - First line astern (Premier centre arrière), Snowbirds 5 - Second line astern (Deuxième centre arrière), Snowbirds 6 - Outer right wing (Ailier droit extérieur), Snowbirds 7 - Outer left wing (Ailier gauche extérieur), Snowbirds 8 - Opposing solo (Solo opposé), Snowbirds 9 - Lead solo Premier solo), Snowbirds 10 - Team coordinator (Coordinateur d'Équipe).

AERONAUTICA MILITARE ITALIANA

FRECCE TRICOLORI

Sion, Switzerland, June 1986.
Downward bomb burst.
Nikon F3P, 180 mm, 1/250 sec.,
F4+2/3, PKM.

Rivolto Airbase, Italy, June 1986.
Number 6 (first slot) aircraft.
Nikon F3P, 180 mm, 1/125 sec.,
F8+1/3, PKM.

Rivolto Airbase, Italy, June 1985.
Take-off roll as seen from Number 4 aircraft (2nd left wingman).
Nikon F3P, 25-50 mm Zoom,
1/250 sec., F5.6+1/2, PKM.

Abbotsford, Canada, August 1986.
Cardioid break.
Nikon F3P, 20 mm, 1/250 sec.,
F5.6+2/3, PKM.

Sion, Switzerland, June 1986.
"Arizona" break.
Nikon F3P, 180 mm, 1/500 sec.,
F4+2/3, PKM.

Abbotsford, Canada, August 1986.
Formation looping in triangle as seen from Number 9 (second slot).
Nikon F3P, 25-50 mm Zoom,
1/250 sec., F6+1/2, PKM.

Rivolto Airbase, Italy, April 1986.
Aircraft moving into line astern.
Nikon F3P, 180 mm, 1/500 sec.,
F2.8+2/3, PKM.

Between Rome and Rimini, June 1985.
Line abreast.
Nikon F3P, 50 mm, 1/125 sec.,
F8+1/2, PKM.

Rivolto Airbase, Italy, June 1985.
Join-up after take-off.
Nikon F3P, 25-50 mm Zoom,
1/125 sec., F8, PKM.

Abbotsford, Canada, August 1986.
Aft section entry in the bull's-eye loop.
Nikon F3P, 20 mm, 1/250 sec.,
F5.6+1/2, PKM.

Between Rimini and Rivolto, Italy, June 1985.
Diamond nine formation.
Nikon F3P, 50 mm, 1/200 sec.,
F5.6+1/2, PKM.

Leeuwarden, The Netherlands, June 1986.
Final fly-by, with colored smoke and gears down. The solo approaches to fly beneath the formation.
Nikon F3T, 300 mm, 1/250 sec.,
F5.6, PKR.

Klagenfurt AP, Austria, August 1984.
Solo exits from the lomçovák.
Nikon F3T, 400 mm, 1/500 sec.,
F5.6+2/3, KR.

Rivolto Airbase, Italy, May 1985.
Nine ships diamond loop.
Nikon F3P, 50 mm, 1/250 sec.,
F5.6+1/2, PKM.

ROYAL AIR FORCE
RED ARROWS

RAF Akrotiri, Cyprus, April 1986.
Nine aircraft in an arrow loop.
Nikon F3P, 25-50 mm Zoom,
1/250 sec., F5.6+2/3, PKM.

RAF Mildenhall, U.K., May 1982.
Taxiing for take-off on runway.
Nikon F2, 200 mm, 1/250 sec.,
F5.6, KM.

RAF Scampton, U.K., September
1986.
Roll-backs.
Nikon F3P, 50 mm, 1/250 sec.,
F2.8+1/2, PKM.

RAF Akrotiri, Cyprus, April 1986.
Roll-backs, with colored smoke.
Nikon F3P, 180 mm, 1/500 sec.,
F4+1/2, PKM.

RAF Mildenhall, U.K., May 1982.
Caterpillar loop.
Nikon F3, 300 mm, 1/500 sec.,
F8, KR.

RAF Scampton, U.K., September
1986.
Caterpillar loop.
Nikon F3P, 25-50 mm Zoom,
1/125 sec., F5.6+1/2, PKR.

Duxford Air Show, U.K., Septem-
ber 1986.
Parasol break (downward bomb
burst).
Nikon F3P, 180 mm, 1/250 sec.,
F5.6+1/2.

RAF Greenham Common, U.K.,
July 1983.
International Air Tattoo "Half
Swan", turning right.
Nikon F3T, 300 mm, 1/500 sec.,
F5.6+2/3, KR.

RAF Farnborough, U.K., Septem-
ber 1986.
Diamond nine formation turning
left.
Nikon F3T, 300 mm, 1/500 sec.,
F5.6+1/2, PKR.

RAF Mildenhall, U.K., May 1982.
Synchro pair cross-over.
Nikon F3, 400 mm, 1/500 sec.,
F5.6+2/3, KR.

RAF Akrotiri, Cyprus, April 1986.
Nine arrow loop.
Nikon F3P, 50 mm, 1/250 sec.,
F5.6+1/2, PKM.

RAF Greenham Common, U.K.
July 1983.
Caterpillar loop entry.
Nikon F3, 300 mm, 1/500 sec.,
F5.6+1/2, KR.

RAF Greenham Common, United
Kingdom, July 1983.
Seven arrow formation turning
left.
Nikon F3, 300 mm, 1/500 sec.,
F5.6+2/3, KR

Akrotiri Bay, Cyprus, April 1986.
On top of the loop in Apollo for-
mation.
Nikon F3P, 50 mm, 1/250 sec.,
F5.6+2/3, PKM.

RAF Akrotiri, Cyprus, April 1986.
Out of a diamond nine loop.
Nikon F3P, 50 mm, 1/250 sec.,
F5.6+1/2, PKM.

U.S. NAVY
BLUE ANGELS

NAF El Centro, California (USA),
March 1987.
A diamond four fly-over.
Nikon F3T, 400 mm, 1/500 sec.,
F8, PKR.

MCAS Yuma, Arizona (USA),
April 1987.
Pilots marching to their aircraft.
Nikon F3T, 300 mm, 1/500 sec.,
F5.6+2/3, PKR.

NAF El Centro, California (USA),
Febraury 1987.
Ready to start engines.
Nikon F3P, 180 mm, 1/250 sec.,
F5.6+1/3, PKM.

NAF El Centro, California (USA),
February 1987.
Reflections on the F-18A Hornet.
Pentax 645, 45 mm, 1/15 sec.,
F5.6, PKR.

NAF El Centro, California (USA),
February 1987.
Taxiing for take-off.
Nikon F3P, 180 mm, 1/250 sec.,
F5.6, PKM.

NAS Pensacola, Florida (USA)
November 1987.
Take-off of number 6 solo air-
craft, which will soon be rolled.
Nikon F3T, 400 mm, 1/500 sec.,
F6+1/2, PKR.

NAF El Centro, California (USA),
February 1987.
Loop by Number 5.
Nikon F3P, 500 mm, 1/250 sec.,
F5.6+2/3, PKM.

NAS Cecil Field, Florida (USA),
May 1987.
Line-abreast loop.
Nikon F3T, 400 mm, 1/500 sec.,
F5.6+2/3, PKR.

NAF El Centro, California (USA),
April 1987.
Delta formation over California
desert.
Pentax 645, 75 mm, 1/250 sec.,
F8+2/3, PKR.

NAF El Centro, California (USA),
March 1987.
The Fortus - Number 5 (inverter)
and Number 6 with landing gear,
flaps, and tailhooks.
Nikon F3T, 300 mm, 1/500 sec.,
F5.6+2/3, PKR.

NAF El Centro, California (USA),
March 1987.
Fan break.
Nikon F3T, 400 mm, 1/500 sec.,
F5.6+2/3, PKR.

NAS Cecil Field, Florida (USA),
May 1987.
Delta vertical break with six air-
craft.
Nikon F3T, 400 mm, 1/500 sec.,
F5.6+2/3, PKR.

U.S.
AIR FORCE
THUNDERBIRDS

Indian Springs, AFB, Nevada (USA), March 1983.
Four aircraft in diamond formation.
Nikon F3T, 400 mm, 1/500 sec., F8, PKR.

Nellis AFB, Nevada (USA), February 1983.
Interior of General Dynamics F-16A "Fighting Falcon" cockpit.
Nikon F3P, 25-50 mm Zoom, 1/30 sec., F8, PKM.

Nellis AFB, Nevada (USA), February 1983.
Reflections on aircraft skin inside the maintenance hangar.
Nikon F3T, 300 mm, 1/60 sec., F5.6, PKR.

George AFB, California (USA), October 1983.
F-16As being towed.
Nikon F3T, 300 mm, 1/250 sec., F8+2/3, PKR.

George AFB, California (USA), October 1983.
One minute to go.
Nikon F3T, 300 mm, 1/500 sec., F5.6+2/3, PKR.

Nellis AFB, Nevada (USA), February 1983.
Taxiing on runway.
Nikon F3T, 400 mm, 1/500 sec., F5.6+1/2, PKR.

Stead AP, Nevada (USA), September 1984.
Looping.
Nikon F3T, 400 mm, 1/500 sec., F5.6+2/3, PKR.

Nellis AFB, Nevada (USA), February 1985.
Number 4 moving to slot position after take-off.
Nikon F3T, 400 mm, 1/500 sec., F5.6+2/3, PKR.

Luke AFB, Arizona (USA), May 1983.
Fly-past in a diamond four with gears down. An aircraft passes on the right at high speed.
Nikon F3T, 300 mm, 1/500 sec., F8, PKR.

Forth Worth, Texas (USA), June 1983.
In-flight refueling as seen from the KC-135 Stratotanker.
Nikon F3P, 20 mm, 1/250 sec., F5.6+1/3, PKM.

Forth Worth, Texas (USA), June 1983.
In-flight refueling as seen from the KC-135 Stratotanker.
Nikon F3P, 85 mm, 1/250 sec., F5.6+1/3, PKM.

Forth Worth, Texas (USA), June 1983.
Leader and slot, in close trail, approach the photographer's aircraft.
Nikon F3P, 25-50 mm Zoom, 1/250 sec., F5.6+1/3, PKM.

RAF Upper Heyford, U.K., June 1984.
Number 5 (inverted) and Number 6 fly-past.
Nikon F3T, 1/400 mm, 1/500 sec., F5.6+2/3, PKR.

RAF Upper Heyford, U.K., June 1984.
Upward bomb burst.
Nikon F3T, 400 mm, 1/500 sec., F8, PKR.

Kadena AB, Japan, October 1983.
Out of a loop.
Nikon F3T, 400 mm, 1/500 sec., F8, PKR.

ARMÉE DE L'AIR
PATROUILLE DE FRANCE

Abbotsford IAP, Canada, August 1986.
Arrow & loop.
Nikon F3P, 25-50 mm Zoom, 1/250 sec., F5.6+2/3, PKM.

Luxembourg IAP, July 1987.
Formation landing.
Pentax 645, 75 mm, 1/250 sec., F8+1/2, PKR.

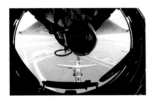

Over Provence, France, June 1987.
Mirror formation flown by the two solos.
Nikon F3P, 16 mm, 1/60 sec., F5.6, PKM.

Over the Mediterranean Sea, France, June 1987.
A diamond eight in a left turn.
Pentax 645, 75 mm, 1/250 sec., F11, PKM.

Vantaa IAP, Finland, August 1983.
Cross-over by the two solos.
Nikon F3T, 400 mm, 1/250 sec., F8+2/3, KR.

RAF Greenham Common, U.K., International Air Tattoo, July 1983.
Cross-over of the two sections, four aircraft each.
Nikon F3T, 300 mm, 1/500 sec., F5.6+2/3, KR.

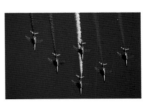

Abbotsford IAP, Canada, August 1986.
Horizontal bomb burst.
Nikon F3T, 400 mm, 1/500 sec., F5.6+2/3, PKR.

Abbotsford IAP, Canada, August 1986.
Looping in arrow formation.
Nikon F3P, 25-50 mm Zoom, 1/250 sec., F5.6+2/3, PKM.

Abbotsford IAP, Canada, August 1986.
Six aircraft in a downward bomb burst.
Nikon F3T, 400 mm, 1/500 sec., F5.6+2/3, PKR.

Vantaa IAP, Finland, August 1983.
Out of the loop in triangle formation.
Nikon F3T, 400 mm, 1/500 sec., F5.6+2/3, KR.

Over Toulouse, France, June 1986.
Concorde formation in a left turn.
Nikon F3P, 25-50 mm Zoom, 1/125 sec., F8+1/8, PKM.

Abbotsford IAP, Canada, August 1986.
On top of the loop in diamond formation.
Nikon F3P, 50 mm, 1/250 sec., Nikon F3P, 50 mm, 1/250 sec., F5.6+1/2, PKM.

Sion, Switzerland, June 1982.
Arrow formation with tri-colored smoke.
Nikon F3, 400 mm, 1/500 sec., F5.6+1/2, PKR.

Over Provence, France, June 1987.
Eight jets in a right echelon.
Nikon F3P, 25-50 mm Zoom, 1/250 sec., F5.6+1/3, PKM.

JAPAN AIR
SELF DEFENCE FORCE

BLUE IMPULSE

Iruma AB, Japan, November 1985.
Delta formation roll, with colored smoke.
Nikon F3T, 400 mm, 1/500 sec., F5.6+2/3, PKR.

Misawa AB, Japan, September 1987.
Pre-flight checks.
Nikon F3P, 300 mm, 1/250 sec., F8+1/2, PKR.

Misawa AB, Japan, September 1987.
Taxiing with landing lights on.
Nikon F3P, 180 mm, 1/250 sec., F5.6+1/3, PKM.

Iruma AB, Japan, November 1982.
Solo roll with white smoke.
Nikon F3T, 400 mm, 1/500 sec., F5.6 1/2, KR.

Nyutabaru AB, Japan, November 1985.
Take-off.
Nikon F3T, 400 mm, 1/500 sec., F5.6+2/3, PKR.

Matsushima AB, Japan, May 1982.
Take-off.
Nikon F3, 400 mm, 1/500 sec., F5.6+2/3, KR.

Nyutabaru AB, Japan, November 1985.
Delta loop.
Nikon F3T, 400 mm, 1/500 sec., F5.6+1/2, PKR.

Iruma AB, Japan, November 1985.
Out of the delta loop.
Nikon F3T, 400 mm, 1/500 sec., F5.6+2/3, PKR.

Yokota AB, Japan, October 1985.
Fly-past in delta formation.
Nikon F3T, 400 mm, 1/500 sec., F5.6+1/2, PKR.

Yokota AB, Japan, October 1985.
Out of the double cloverleaf in arrow formation.
Nikon F3T, 300 mm, 1/500 sec., F5.6+2/3, PKR.

Iruma AB, Japan, November 1983.
Entering the loop in a line abreast.
Nikon F3T, 400 mm, 1/500 sec., F5.6+1/2, PKR.

Misawa, Japan, September 1987.
Upward bomb burst.
Nikon F3T, 400 mm, 1/500 sec., F5.6+2/3, PKR.

Iruma AB, Japan, November 1985.
Tuck-over break.
Nikon F3T, 300 mm, 1/250 sec., F8, PKR.

CANADIAN ARMED FORCES

SNOWBIRDS

Over Vancouver Island, Canada, April 1982.
Left turn in a nine aircraft diamond.
Nikon F2, 50 mm, 1/125 sec., F8, KM.

CFB Comox, Canada, April 1982.
Ready to start up the engines.
Nikon F2, 200 mm, 1/250 sec., F6+1/3, KM.

CFB Comox, Canada, April 1982.
Taxiing on the runway.
Nikon F3P, 180 mm, 1/250 sec., F4+1/2, PKM.

In Reno, Nevada (USA), September 1983. - Number 9 as seen from Number 5.
Nikon F2, 20 mm, 1/125 sec., F5.6 1/2, KM.

Over Vancouver Island, Canada, April 1982.
A "V"formation in a 45°-banked left turn, with lead solo inverted.
Nikon F2, 50 mm, 1/250 sec., F5.6+1/2, KM.

Over Vancouver Island, Canada, April 1982.
Coming out of a loop in a diamond nine formation.
Nikon F2, 28 mm, 1/250 sec., F5.6+2/3, KM.

Over the Pacific Ocean, Canada, April 1986.
Corcorde formation.
Nikon F2, 28 mm, 1/250 sec., F5.6+2/3, KM.

Over Vancouver Island, Canada, April 1986.
Knife-edge turn in a diamond nine.
Nikon F2, 50 mm, 1/250 sec., F5.6, KM.

CFB Moose Jaw, Canada, June 1984. - Snowbirds 8, 9, and 5 split in front of the crowd.
Nikon F3, 400 mm, 1/500 sec., F5.6+2/3, PKR.

Over Vancouver Island, Canada, April 1986. - On a top of a loop, in a diamond nine formation.
Nikon F2, 50 mm, 1/250 sec., F5.6+1/2, KM.

Over Vancouver Island, Canada, April 1986.
Out of a loop.
Nikon F3P, 25-50 mm Zoom, 1/250 sec., F5.6+1/2, PKM.

Over Vancouver Island, Canada, April 1982. An arrow formation.
Nikon F2, 50 mm, 1/250 sec., F5.6, KM.

Stead AP, Nevada (USA), September 1985. Downward bomb
Nikon F3T, 300 mm, 1/500 sec., F8, PKR.

PRINTED IN ITALY ▥ GRAFICHE LEMA - MANIAGO/PN